JOHN SIEBELING

Request for information should be addressed to:

John Siebeling Ministries, 650 Houston Hill Road, Eads, TN 38028

ISBN-13: 978-0-615-38861-8

Printed in the United States of America.

johnsiebeling.com

CONTENTS

Have You Made a Fresh Start?

HAVE YOU MADE A FRESH START?

2 Corinthians 5:17 – *"Now we look inside, and what we see is that anyone united with the Messiah gets a fresh start, is created new. The old life is gone; a new life burgeons!"* (MSG)

What an awesome promise! After nearly 30 years of pastoring and leading people, I never grow tired of watching individuals make a fresh start with God. In every service at our church, and at the close of every one of our television programs, it's always my highest honor to open the door for people to begin a relationship with God.

God loves you and me so much that He gave His only Son, Jesus Christ. The Bible says that Jesus came in the form of a man and walked this earth, the same earth we're walking today. He was tempted in every way so He could fully relate to us, but He never gave in to the temptation, and therefore, lived a sinless life. He became the sacrifice for our sins by dying on the cross. Every single thing we have ever done wrong, every mistake, all of our sin – past, present, future – was placed on Jesus. He took our punishment on the cross and was crucified. He was laid in a tomb and three days later, by the power of the Holy Spirit, He rose from the dead. He overcame our sin!

The Bible teaches that through the cross, we receive forgiveness from our sin, and through His resurrection, we have new life and a new beginning – a fresh start.

Romans 10:9-10 – *"...if you confess with your mouth, 'Jesus is Lord,' and believe in your heart that God raised him from the dead, you will be saved. For it is with your heart that you believe and are justified, and it is with your mouth that you confess and are saved."*

These verses give us the practical steps to a fresh start with God. It starts with believing. In our heart, we believe the story I just described. We believe God loves us and sent Jesus. We believe that Jesus gave His life on the cross and rose from the dead. We may not fully understand it all, but something inside our heart says, "This is true." When we believe in our heart, then we can "confess" or pray with our mouth. We pray and declare our love for God and invite His presence into our lives. From that moment, our lives are changed! The Bible says we are "saved", meaning we're united with God through Jesus Christ.

The word "saved" is a Bible word. You may have never heard it, or maybe it carries some baggage for you. It simply means "to be pulled out." I always tell people to picture themselves in a war zone, in the middle of a firefight, buildings on fire, nothing but chaos. You're standing there, defenseless, not sure what to do. Then all of a sudden you hear a helicopter overhead and out of nowhere a rope ladder comes down and rescues you. Picture that from a spiritual perspective. That's what it means to be saved. We're rescued from an eternity spent in darkness and saved from a purposeless life on earth. Another word the Bible uses to describe what happens when we receive Jesus into our lives is "salvation."

I'm not sure where you are on your journey. Maybe you don't ever remember praying a prayer asking God for forgiveness and inviting Jesus into your life. Many people I meet don't ever recall making that decision. You may have been to church or read your Bible, but those things don't make you a Christian. You become a Christian when you choose to accept Jesus – when you believe in your heart and pray with your mouth. It could be that at some point in your life you did pray and receive Jesus, but if you were to be honest, today your life isn't on track with God. You might have made some choices that caused you to fall away from a relationship with God. Maybe even unintentionally, over time, you have just drifted away and you know in your heart you need to renew your relationship with God.

The great news is that God stands before us with arms wide open. The Bible says that He loves us with an everlasting love, which means His love never ends! He can – and will – forgive you of anything you ask. I encourage you, if you're reading this right now and you are insecure or unsure of where you stand in your relationship with God, take a minute and pray this prayer:

God, thank you for the amazing plan you have for my life. I come today to ask you to fill me with your presence. Thanks for sending your Son, Jesus, to die on a cross for me so I could receive forgiveness from my sin. Thank you for raising Jesus from the dead so I could have a new life. I ask you to forgive me of my sin, cleanse me and make me new. Come live inside of me and give me the strength to live for you. In Jesus' name, amen.

There you go! You just made a fresh start with God. One of my favorite verses describing the fresh start process is Colossians 1:13, *"For he has rescued us from the kingdom of darkness and transferred us into the Kingdom of his dear Son..."* (NLT). It's pretty amazing to think that a spiritual "transaction" has just happened. Your life is now in God's hands.

It's just the first step, but it is a step. I want to encourage you to keep reading and learn as much as you can about building a great relationship with God. Here's how I designed this booklet: I thought about some of the most important things that have helped me in my relationship with God, and I wrote a short chapter about each one. There are a lot of things I could have written about, but I chose seven so that you can read one chapter each day. By the end of the week, you can have a strong start on your journey living for God. Take some time to look up the key verses at the end of each chapter and answer the questions. I know it will really help you connect into the things of God. Remember, God has an amazing future for you. He loves you and has a good plan for your life!

Letting God Change You

LETTING GOD CHANGE YOU

Now that you've had this amazing spiritual experience of accepting Jesus, it's all about living out that fresh start and beginning to live the way God wants you to live. In this chapter, we'll talk about some foundational principles that will help you start to grow and get your new life in Jesus off to a great start.

Water Baptism

I always encourage every new believer to get water baptized because it's all about letting everyone know you're leaving the old behind and stepping into the new life God has for you.

Water baptism is a way for believers to outwardly express what God has done in their hearts and lives in the presence of other believers. It's kind of like putting a stake in the ground and making a declaration, "The old life is gone, my new life in Christ has begun, and I'm not going back."

Why is baptism is so important? First, in Matthew 28:19-20, Jesus gives his disciples a two-part command: "So, you must go and make disciples of all nations. Baptizing them in the name of the Father and of the Son and of the Holy Spirit." This shows us that it was Jesus' intention that salvation and baptism go together - that if someone receives salvation, baptism is a natural next step.

Second, baptism is the example Jesus set for us in His own life. In Matthew chapter 3 we read about how Jesus asked his cousin, John the Baptist, to baptize Him as He prepared to begin His earthly ministry. It was a spiritually significant moment in His life, and it is in our lives as well.

Finally, when you're baptized in water, it's a public declaration that you are identifying yourself with Jesus. In the Bible, water represents cleansing. As we go under the water, it symbolizes being cleansed from our sin as the old life is buried, just as Jesus was buried after He died to take the punishment for our sins. Coming up out of the water is a demonstration of the new life we have through the power of Jesus' resurrection.

Transformation: The Key to Lasting Change

I'm sure you've noticed that all of your problems didn't just disappear after you prayed that salvation prayer. The truth is, this life you live for God is a journey, and even though you are saved and full of the presence of God, you will now need God's help to transform your life. The Bible teaches that each of us is one person, but we have different aspects of our being. Check out this verse – I think it will explain what I mean…

1 Thessalonians 5:23 – *"May God himself, the God of peace, sanctify you through and through. May your whole spirit, soul and body be kept blameless at the coming of our Lord Jesus Christ."*

So, this verse tells us that we have a spirit, a soul and a body. Our spirit refers to that part of our being where the presence of God resides. When we ask Jesus to forgive us and come live inside of us, He comes to live in our spirit. Our spirit is made alive in Him, but our soul is another story. Our soul is made up of our mind, our emotions and our will. In other words – it's how we think (our mind), how we feel (our emotions) and the choices we make (our will). Sure, we're Christians and we love God and want to please Him, but we now find that there is a conflict on the inside because so many of our thoughts, feelings and desires are in conflict with what God wants for us. Without getting too complicated here, the reality is you and I were born with what the Bible calls a sin nature. Because of the choice Adam and Eve made in the garden, all of us are born apart from God, and therefore, we have a desire to please ourselves. When we make a fresh start, the Bible teaches that we are born again.

John 3:3 – *"In reply Jesus declared, 'I tell you the truth, no one can see the kingdom of God unless he is born again.'"*

When you accept Jesus, a new you is born. The problem is the old you, the sin nature, remains and these two are in conflict.

Galatians 5:17 – *"For the sinful nature desires what is contrary to the Spirit, and the Spirit what is contrary to the sinful nature. They are in conflict with each other, so that you do not do what you want."*

Everyone deals with this conflict. In fact, the Apostle Paul, who was an amazing Christian, great theologian and wrote the majority of the New Testament, struggled with this conflict and wrote about it in the book of Romans.

Romans 7:18-23 –*"And I know that nothing good lives in me, that is, in my sinful nature. I want to do what is right, but I can't. I want to do what is good, but I don't. I don't want to do what is wrong, but I do it anyway. But if I do what I don't want to do, I am not really the one doing wrong; it is sin living in me that does it. I have discovered this principle of life - that when I want to do what is right, I inevitably do what is wrong. I love God's law with all my heart. But there is another power within me that is at war with my mind. This power makes me a slave to the sin that is still within me."* (NLT)

In fact, the Apostle Paul referred to this conflict as "the good fight of faith" because even though it is a conflict, it is a good one! We're in this conflict because we're going through the process of becoming more like God. Make no mistake, when you accept Jesus you become a Christian – you're on your way to heaven. That is the salvation experience, and in a sense, it is the easiest step to take because Jesus paid the price for you. All you have to do is receive. However, there is a price you have to pay, and it requires you offering yourself to God so He can change you and use you to impact other people.

Remember, the part God wants to change is our soul. That means the way we think, the way we feel and our choices. Remember this verse from 1 Thessalonians:

1 Thessalonians 5:23 – *"May God himself, the God of peace, sanctify you through and through. May your whole spirit, soul and body be kept blameless at the coming of our Lord Jesus Christ."*

There are a few things that I want you to notice about this verse. First, it is God himself who changes us. We can't change ourselves. Have you ever tried to break a bad habit? It's a tough thing to do. Make sure your focus is on God, press into Him and you will find that He will start changing you. If you focus on your problem, or how you feel about something, then you will become frustrated. Focus on God. He is the one who is going to change you.

Secondly, notice it says that He is "the God of peace." The process of becoming like God doesn't have to be an anxious, frustrating process. We can make it like that if we're not careful. God is a God of peace. He loves you and He has an awesome, beautiful plan for your life. He is going to keep leading you and changing you so that you become more like Him. God's work of change in your life flourishes when you learn to relax, stay in a peaceful place and let Him have His way in your life.

Thirdly, notice that God is thorough. He wants to sanctify or change you "through and through." In other words, He wants to change you so that you never go backward. He's an "all the way" God, working carefully and completely to transform your life.

How does God bring change? When I think about how God changes me, I always come back to three things, and I think these are the three most important spiritual change agents in our lives.

God's Word

The Bible is God's Word to us. It is our ultimate authority for life and godliness, and it is the greatest tool in God's hand to bring change into our lives.

Romans 12:1-2 – *"Therefore, I urge you, brothers, in view of God's mercy, to offer your bodies as living sacrifices, holy and pleasing to God – this is your spiritual act of worship. Do not conform any longer to the pattern of this world, but be transformed by the renewing of your mind. Then you will be able to test and approve what God's will is – his good, pleasing and perfect will."*

I think this is such a great passage that speaks right to what we've been talking about in this chapter. First, we offer ourselves to God and make a fresh start with Him. Second, just as soon as we offer our lives, we begin to sense that God wants us to live a new way – "not conforming any longer to the pattern of this world." We're convicted about some things in our life that need to change. Thirdly, we start to see the changes come as our mind changes. Then we begin to know and to walk in God's will for our lives. That third step is the one I want you to really think about: renewing our mind. As we see in Romans 12:2, our lives are transformed (changed) when we renew our mind. That means in order to see change happen in our lives, we have to get rid of old thought patterns and start thinking in a new way. What we put into our minds is so important because it determines what comes out in the other areas of our lives. The results show up in our words, our feelings, our actions and our attitudes toward God, ourselves and others.

Ephesians 4:23 – *"...be made new in the attitude of your minds."*

If you're not happy with what's coming out, take a look at what you're putting in. What are you listening to on the radio on the way to work? What are you watching on TV before you go to bed? What kind of conversations are you having with friends? What are you reading? They may not even be "bad" things, but consider the kind of messages that you're putting into your mind. Are they taking your life where you want to go? There are some things in our lives that we will continue to struggle with or be held back by until we overcome the wrong thinking that is the root issue of the problem. Renewing our minds is the key to experiencing a life filled with the freedom, wholeness and peace that God intends for us. The most powerful tool in renewing our minds and breaking free from old thinking patterns is God's Word.

Hebrews 4:12 tells us, *"For the word of God is alive and powerful. It is sharper than the sharpest two-edged sword, cutting between soul and spirit, between joint and marrow. It exposes our innermost thoughts and desires."* (NLT)

Even though men wrote the Bible, the Holy Spirit is really the author. He guided and inspired them with what and how to write. Now, even though it is thousands of years later, when we read the Bible the Holy Spirit illuminates the Word to us. That means He's the one who enables our hearts and minds to understand it. When you read the Bible, you are literally sitting down with the author, getting His thoughts on what is written. In other words, the Holy Spirit takes the Word and uses it to speak right to us, to our situations and circumstances. That's amazing! And that's why you should read the Bible every day. It has a cleansing and empowering effect on our lives.

God's People

When I think of how God has changed me, the impact on my life through relationships has been enormous. My life has changed because of the people God has brought into my world.

One of the most important things we can do is open our lives to the right people and let them teach us, encourage us and give us advice. Our lives will be better for it. You can't open your life to everyone, but you need to submit your life in two ways. First, to the pastors and leaders of your local church. Second, to Christian friends who are on the journey with you and are headed in the same direction.

Hebrews 13:17 – *"Obey your leaders and submit to their authority. They keep watch over you as men who must give an account. Obey them so that their work will be a joy, not a burden, for that would be of no advantage to you."*

Ephesians 5:21 – *"Submit to one another out of reverence for Christ."*

God's Voice

The Bible teaches that Jesus is our Shepherd and we are His sheep. He is constantly speaking to us and leading us.

John 10:4 – *"When he has brought out all his own, he goes on ahead of them, and his sheep follow him because they know his voice."*

When I talk about God's voice, it's not something scary or mystical. God speaks to us by the Holy Spirit in our heart. Sometimes it's like we're hearing a whisper in our heart, other times it is just a sense or conviction of what we're supposed to do, something we shouldn't do or something we should stop doing.

Remember He is the God of peace and He is a friend that sticks closer than a brother. He knows exactly what we need. He leads us into, out of and through all kinds of different situations. He is always leading us, and His leading brings change. God's voice will never contradict His Word. He will never ask you to do something that doesn't agree with what the Bible says.

One final thought: keep in mind that in order to grow spiritually, we need to be free. Spiritual freedom brings spiritual maturity. It comes as we allow God to change and transform our lives through His Word, His people and His voice. Don't get discouraged if you feel like things are happening too slowly. Transformation doesn't happen overnight. Becoming more like Jesus is a journey that you will be on for the rest of your life. Stay submitted to the process and allow God to do all that He wants to do in and through you. God is in control and He is working in your life, even if you can't see it or feel it. Commit to doing your part and I can assure you God will do His!

Philippians 1:6 – *"...being confident of this, that he who began a good work in you will carry it on to completion until the day of Christ Jesus."*

Key Scriptures

Psalm 119:9-11
Psalm 119:45
John 3:3
John 10:4
Romans 7:18-23
Romans 12:1-2
Galatians 5:17
Ephesians 4:23
Ephesians 5:21
Philippians 1:6
1 Thessalonians 5:23

Hebrews 4:12

Hebrews 13:17

Questions

1. In what areas of your life do you need God to bring change?

2. Does your view of God line up with what you read about Him in the Bible?

3. What are some specific ways of thinking that you need to change?

4. A life-giving church and healthy church leaders are some of the greatest catalysts for change in our lives. What practical steps do you need to take to make church a priority and open your life to leaders and friends that can help you grow wiser and stronger?

Confidence in Your New Life

CONFIDENCE IN YOUR NEW LIFE

Hebrews 10:35 – *"So do not throw away your confidence; it will be richly rewarded."*

Godly confidence is a great gift. I'm not referring to an arrogant, self-centered type of confidence, but rather a spiritual confidence: knowing in your heart who God is, who He says you are and what He can do in and through you.

In Philippians 3:3, the Bible says that we should put "no confidence in the flesh," which literally means we really can't be confident at all in who we are in our own strength. Our confidence has to be in God and in Him alone. Let's take a few minutes and think about some specific things about God that you need to be confident in.

Be Confident That God Forgives Anything and Everything

Probably one of the greatest sources of frustration, discouragement and even fear in the lives of many Christians is mistakes made in their past. *Am I really forgiven?* This is a question that I get so often. The answer is YES! If you've asked God to forgive you, then you are forgiven! God not only has the capacity to forgive you and cleanse you, He also has the desire and the willingness to forgive you.

1 John 1:9 – *"If we confess our sins, he is faithful and just and will forgive us our sins and purify us from all unrighteousness."*

It's not only the past that He forgives, but He is also ready to forgive you anytime that you stumble or fall. He knows we're not perfect and though we strive to walk in purity, there are those times when we sin and fall short of God's best. I believe that it's in those moments when our relationship with God is truly tested. Too often, when we fail, we tend to pull back and think, *What good will it do to keep asking God to forgive me?* The truth is, sin is destructive and there are always consequences when we make bad decisions and give in to temptation, just like there are positive benefits and great things that flow in to our lives when we make good decisions. To pull back from God when we've failed is not what He wants. He loves you and wants to help you. He will forgive you when you ask, and as you keep walking with God, He will give you the strength to keep getting up and moving forward.

Proverbs 24:16 – *"For though a righteous man falls seven times, he rises again..."*

Be Confident in Who God Is and What He's Done for You

When we pray and accept Jesus, asking Him to forgive

us, we are accepted by God and we become His children. The Bible calls us "sons and daughters of God," which is pretty amazing. I know some people didn't have a great upbringing and maybe their father was not involved, or worse, was neglectful or abusive, but God is a good father. He loves us and cares for us and wants the best for us. The thing that we need to keep in mind is that we are His children and He will never disown us or leave us. There is nothing more that we can do to earn God's approval.

I believe there is a huge difference between Christianity and religion. That might sound confusing to you, but keep reading. Religion is a system of beliefs that explain God. I realize many people categorize Christianity as a religion, but in the purest sense, Christianity isn't really a religion at all because it is based on a relationship. As a matter of fact, if you try to build a relationship with Jesus in a religious way, you'll find yourself loaded down. Let me explain this in a better way by comparing religion and Christianity.

Religion is spelled DO
Christianity is spelled DONE

Every religion in the world can be summarized in one of two words – "do" or "done." Religion says, "Here's what you have to do to get God to like you," followed by a list of things you should and should not do. If you work the list and get it all right, God will smile and you're ok.

But Jesus came and basically said, "No. That's all wrong. That's not it – I want to know you and I want you to know me. It's not religion; it's relationship. I've already done everything so we can get to know one another. You don't have to do, do, do. You just have to accept what I've already done!"

There are really two paths you can choose in your relationship with God. The first is to spend the rest of your life trying to earn God's approval by your own efforts, doing or not doing certain things. This is a very hard path because we can never be perfect and will end up falling short, feeling condemned and far from God. The second is to enjoy God's approval by accepting what Jesus Christ has already done. You can't earn God's love, acceptance and approval. You already have it! We desire to live a life that pleases God because of His love for us and our relationship with Him.

Religion is man's attempt to reach God
Christianity is God reaching out to man

Religion says, "Get your act together and God will accept you." Christianity is Jesus saying, "Come to me and I'll help you get your act together."

Romans 5:8 – *"Christ arrives right on time...He didn't, and doesn't, wait for us to get ready. He presented himself for this sacrificial death when we were far too weak and rebellious to do anything to get ourselves ready."* (MSG)

Religion focuses on the external
Christianity focuses on the internal

Religion is all about behavior modification: correct your behavior, follow certain rules, and stay in line. The problem is that behavior modification can only get us so far and it doesn't produce life on the inside. It produces fear of external consequences.

Something has to happen on the inside. Instead of just being afraid of the external consequences, we need to have a change of heart.

1 Samuel 16:7 – *"...The Lord does not look at the things man looks at. Man looks at the outward appearance, but the Lord looks at the heart."*

This is the essence of Christianity: a change of heart. Jesus has the power to change us on the inside. The only problem is many people don't see Christianity that way; they see Christianity in a religious way, making it all about what you can or can't do. However, that's not true Christianity. When we allow God to change our heart, right thoughts and right actions will naturally follow.

Religion is based on knowledge
Christianity is based on life

The goal of Christianity isn't to know the Bible more. The goal of Christianity is to experience the Bible more! God doesn't want us to just know about Him, God wants us to actually know Him. There's a huge difference in knowing about someone and actually knowing them. You can know everything there is to know about a celebrity or famous athlete but that hardly means that you know them or have a relationship with them. It's the same way with God – we can know a lot about Him, but it doesn't necessarily mean that we know Him. Listen to Jesus as He confronts some religious people...

John 5:39-40 – *"You diligently study the Scriptures because you think that by them you possess eternal life. These are the Scriptures that testify about me, yet you refuse to come to me to have life."*

When we have a relationship with Him, we have an understanding of His character and heart toward us. He has an active place in our lives that makes a difference in how we live. When we truly know God, we fall more in love with Him and can't help but be transformed as we encounter His presence in our lives.

Remember, God is your father. He loves you and through Jesus Christ you can have a relationship with Him. You need to feel the freedom and the confidence to enjoy your relationship with God. Ephesians 3:12 tells us, *"In him and through faith in him we may approach God with freedom and confidence."*

Be Confident of Who You Are in Christ

Our confidence needs to be in God, not in ourselves. The biggest part of being confident in God is being confident in His Word, the Bible. God's Word plays an incredible role in our lives. When it comes to building you up and strengthening your life on the inside, nothing can replace it. Being spiritually confident means knowing what the Bible says about you.

When I first became a Christian, someone gave me a sheet of paper that had a list of scriptures with a short prayer beside each one. The prayer was a confession taken from the verse. I was encouraged to look up the verses one at a time to see what they said. Then everyday I read those short prayers, and confessed them over my life. That little exercise turned into a powerful spiritual discipline for me. It helped me learn the Bible and build a strong framework of the right spiritual identity in my life. I've listed a few confessions out for you. Take some time, look up the verses in your Bible and start praying these thoughts over your life.

- I am the light of the world.
  Matthew 5:14
- I am the righteousness of God in Jesus Christ.
  2 Corinthians 5:21
- I am holy and without blame before Him in love.
  Ephesians 1:3-14
- I am greatly loved by God.
  Ephesians 2:4, Colossians 3:12
- I am alive with Christ.
  Ephesians 2:4-5
- I am created in Christ to do good works.
  Ephesians 2:10

- I have the peace of God that passes understanding. Philippians 4:7
- I can do all things through Christ Jesus. Philippians 4:13
- I am made strong by His power. Colossians 1:11
- I am whole and complete in Him. Colossians 2:10

Key Scriptures

1 Samuel 16:7

Proverbs 24:16

John 5:39-40

Romans 5:8

Ephesians 3:12

Philippians 1:6

Philippians 2:13

Philippians 3:3

Hebrews 4:16

Hebrews 10:35

1 John 1:9

Questions

1. Which of the previous "I am..." statements most challenges your current thoughts about who you are?

2. Do you have mindsets, perspectives or even habits that are rooted in "religion" rather than "relationship"?

3. Which area of spiritual confidence do you need to grow in most (confidence that God forgives anything and everything, confidence in who God is and what He's done for you, or confidence about who you are in Christ)?

Thriving in God's House

THRIVING IN GOD'S HOUSE

As you're laying the foundation in your new life with Christ, one of the most important things to do is find a life-giving local church and get connected through attending and serving each week. One of the reasons I'm so passionate about this is that the local church has played a huge role in my personal journey as a Christian. It was through getting planted in a local church that I began to understand what it really meant to be a Christian, grow in my relationship with Christ and get a vision for my life. I love the local church. I love going to church. I love building the local church. Nothing makes me happier than when I see other people fall in love with the local church and watch their lives begin to flourish.

Another reason I'm passionate about the Church is because God is passionate about His Church. It's His treasure, His pride and joy. In Ephesians, Paul draws the parallel between Jesus' love for the Church and the love a husband has for his bride. We can't say we love Jesus but don't really like the Church. Jesus loved the Church so much that He gave His life for it.

Jesus established His Church and there is no institution, no government, no social justice movement or political regime that can replace the role of the Church in our world.

Matthew 16:18 – *"...upon this rock I will build my church, and all the powers of hell will not conquer it."* (NLT)

The Message translation says it this way:

"...I will put together my church, a church so expansive with energy that not even the gates of hell will be able to keep it out."

That's incredible! The Church is the most powerful vehicle we have for reaching people with the message of Christ and the hope He brings. It's the ultimate cause and it will never fail. I want to align myself with God's purposes and spend my life building what He's building...His Church!

I don't think there's anyone in the Bible who expressed a greater passion for God's House than David. When you read the book of Psalms, which is really like David's diary, his commitment to God's House is evident. When he wrote them, he probably didn't intend for all of us to read them; he was simply pouring his heart out to God. When we read them today, we get a glimpse of what was in his heart concerning the House of God.

David says in Psalm 23:6, *"...I will dwell in the house of the Lord forever."*

Here are a few other translations of this verse:

"...I'm back home in the house of God for the rest of my life." (MSG)

"...and I will live forever in your house, Lord." (CEV)

"...and through the length of my days the house of the Lord [and His presence] shall be my dwelling place!" (AMPC)

As we can see, church was a huge part of David's life. He was incredibly passionate about God's House. Some people might look at these passages about God's House and think, *"Well that was then. How can that be relevant for me?"* A commitment to God's House today carries the same significance and benefits that it always has.

What We Find in God's House

God's Presence

Psalm 26:8 – *"I love your sanctuary, Lord, the place where your glorious presence dwells."* (NLT)

God's Protection

Psalm 27:4-5 – *"One thing I ask of the Lord, this is what I seek: that I may dwell in the house of the Lord all the days of my life...For in the day of trouble he will keep me safe in his dwelling; he will hide me in the shelter of his tabernacle and set me high upon a rock."*

God's Provision

Psalm 36:8 – *"They feast on the abundance of your house..."*

Psalm 84:4 – *"Blessed are those who dwell in your house..."*

Psalm 65:4 – *"...we are filled with the good things of your house..."*

God's House is full of "good things." We build relationships, have opportunities to make a difference, receive encouragement and support, grow spiritually and find contentment knowing that we are living a life of purpose. It is bursting with warmth, generosity, friendships and so many other good things for your life! There is no equal to the blessings, both tangible and intangible, that come into every area of our lives through God's House. His heart toward you overflows with good things and He wants to position you to be able to receive them from Him. So how do we receive all the benefits of God's House in our lives? We find the answer in Psalm 92:12-15:

"The righteous will flourish like a palm tree, they will grow like a cedar of Lebanon; planted in the house of the Lord, they will flourish in the courts of our God. They will still bear fruit in old age, they will stay fresh and green, proclaiming, 'The Lord is upright; he is my Rock, and there is no wickedness in him.'"

We experience the blessings and good things that come from God's House when we are planted there.

What It Means to be Planted in God's House

To be planted means *to set in the soil for growth; to set firmly in position; to establish; to fix firmly*. The analogy used here is that of a garden or a field. Your life is like a seed and the local church is like the ground or the soil. God wants you to be planted in the local church for your spiritual growth!

Without the seed, the soil is pretty much insignificant. Without the soil, the seed is fairly insignificant as well. Together, however, they can produce a crop that can be enjoyed and even used to produce more crops! It is when they come together that they produce something significant that neither could produce on their own. The same is true about our lives and the local church. When we plant ourselves in the local church, it produces something beautiful, productive, powerful and influential.

Here's how it works. The seed has all of the potential. The life isn't in the soil; the life is in the seed. But the seed cannot bring out all of the potential that's inside of it. Only the soil has the ability to draw that life out of the seed. Without the soil, the life that is inside the seed cannot be initiated or sustained. Within every seed there is life, an embryo, and covering the embryo is the outer wall of the seed.

The key to starting the process of growth and germination is creating a change in that outer wall. In most seeds, it's a combination of three things that initiate life - heat, light and moisture. The important thing about the soil is that it has to be strong enough to hold the seed in place. It also must be flexible and loose enough to allow the roots to push out of the bottom and the buds to sprout out of the top. Finally, it must also have the ability to provide the seed the right environment for growth. Think about the spiritual analogy and how that applies to our lives:

The seed represents me and you. We are the seeds, packed with potential and life. God puts it inside of us. He also gives us a divinely implanted sense of purpose. Deep in the core of our being, we yearn to be significant and make a difference with our lives. That sense of significance is put within us by God.

The soil represents the environment and atmosphere of the local church. Remember, the soil holds the seed and allows it to have sustained growth. It's also the source of the key ingredients that are necessary for growth. Just like the soil provides the seed what it needs to grow, a healthy local church provides us with what we need to grow and mature as believers - God's presence, His Word, good relationships, the Holy Spirit and more. In the same way that a seed needs soil in order to grow and produce fruit, we need a local church to grow and become all God wants us to be.

Just like the soil, a local church should be strong enough to hold and sustain us, flexible enough to allow us to grow roots and blossom, and receptive enough to allow God to have His way, moving in the lives of the people, breaking down that outer wall so that life can spring forth.

Jesus talked about this process of planting and growth all the time. Think about these two examples:

In Luke 8:4-8, Jesus tells a story about a man who was scattering seed and the seed fell in four different places. In the first three places, the seed was never truly planted in good ground. The first seed just sat on top of the soil and was eaten by birds. The second seed started to grow, but didn't put its roots down deep, so it withered and died. The third seed was choked by thorns. The last seed, however, was planted in good ground and produced a crop that was exponentially more than what was sown.

Another example Jesus gave about the process of planting is found in John 12:24. He talked about the real key for the seed: the seed has to make a total commitment to the soil. Let's read that passage now in two different versions:

"Listen carefully: Unless a grain of wheat is buried in the ground, dead to the world, it is never any more than a grain of wheat. But if it is buried, it sprouts and

reproduces itself many times over." (MSG)

"I assure you, most solemnly I tell you, Unless a grain of wheat falls into the earth and dies, it remains [just one grain; it never becomes more but lives] by itself alone. But if it dies, it produces many others and yields a rich harvest." (AMPC)

What does all of this mean practically for me and you? It means we need to find a local church that we can truly commit our "all" to. Joining a church, planting your life in a church, is really a powerful thing. In fact, it's the thing that is going to draw that potential, purpose and significance out of your life. That's why choosing where we plant ourselves should be a really strategic decision and not something we take lightly.

Here are a few of the things you should consider when looking for a healthy local church to get planted in:

- Word – God's Word is believed to be the standard and is preached in a way you can understand and apply to your daily life.
- Worship – God's presence is tangible and there is freedom to connect with Him. The style shouldn't be your primary consideration; worship is an attitude and a heart issue.
- Vision – The church is going somewhere. You can

see where it's going and desire to be involved. It values reaching out to and serving the community.

- Leadership – The leaders of the church are strong, committed, humble people with good character.
- Atmosphere – The environment is life-giving, encouraging, fun, friendly and Spirit-filled.

I encourage you to make a decision to get planted in a thriving, life-giving, local church. Maybe you've never been planted in a church before and this is an entirely new concept for you. Maybe you've been committed to a church in the past and invested a lot, only to have a hurtful experience cause you to pull back a little or disconnect from church altogether. I want to challenge you to give "being planted" a chance and see what happens in your life. When we truly get planted in a great church, we experience life and church the way God intended us to. We're rooted in a healthy, loving House, surrounded by a family of believers, growing in a positive, encouraging environment.

Key Scriptures

Jeremiah 17:8

Psalm 23:6

Psalm 26:8

Psalm 27:4-5

Psalm 36:8

Psalm 52:8-9

Psalm 65:4

Psalm 84:4

Psalm 92:12-15

Matthew 16:18

Luke 8:4-8

John 12:24

Questions

1. What areas of your life could benefit and grow as a result of being planted in God's House?

2. What mindsets or thoughts have you had that may have prevented you from being planted in a local church?

3. What is your next step when it comes to getting planted in God's House?

Moving Forward

MOVING FORWARD

I love this quote from Jim Ryun, one of the greatest runners of all time: "Motivation is what gets you started. Habit is what keeps you going." The same is true when it comes to growing in our spiritual lives. Now that you've begun a relationship with God by making a fresh start, it's important that you grow and become strong in your relationship with Him. We do that by establishing habits and disciplines in our lives that nourish and strengthen us spiritually. Those habits and disciplines play a significant role in helping us mature spiritually and become all that God wants us to be.

In this chapter, I want to talk about six key habits that can move every Christian's life forward:

- Reading the Bible
- Praying
- Worshiping
- Fasting
- Giving
- Serving

Reading the Bible

2 Timothy 3:16-17 tells us, *"The whole Bible was given to us by inspiration from God and is useful to*

teach us what is true and to make us realize what is wrong in our lives; it straightens us out and helps us do what is right. It is God's way of making us well prepared at every point, fully equipped to do good to everyone." (TLB)

The Bible is God's instruction manual for our lives. It's so important that we're constantly taking it in because it's how we get to know God, and it's what transforms our lives. When we get to know Him, we experience His divine power and receive everything we need for life and godliness (2 Peter 1:3).

We are spirit-beings who have a soul and live in a body. We feed our physical bodies each day to fuel them so they stay strong and healthy. In the same way, we have to feed our spirits each day with God's Word. In Matthew 4:4 Jesus said, *"...Man does not live on bread alone, but on every word that comes from the mouth of God."*

God's Word guides us, encourages us, strengthens us and helps us grow. It's what refreshes our hearts and transforms our minds. The key to a changed life is a changed mind. Make it a habit to spend time in God's Word every day and it will produce results in your life.

Here are some practical tips about reading the Bible:

- Set aside a specific time each day to read the Bible. Morning is good because it gives God priority in your day and prepares you for the day ahead.
- Deal with any attitudes in your heart that might keep you from receiving from God – anger, unforgiveness, pride, jealousy, etc.
- Open your heart and ask God to speak to you.
- Take notes on what you read.
- Start small and be consistent.
- Try a Bible reading plan or a one-year Bible if you don't know where to start.

Praying

Prayer is another spiritual discipline that is so vital to our spiritual growth. When we pray, we receive direction, strength, comfort, encouragement and so much more. Prayer doesn't have to be fancy or overly spiritual - prayer is simply communicating with God. Communication in a good relationship isn't one-sided. It's interactive, with both sides participating. Part of prayer is us talking to God. The other part of prayer is us hearing from Him. That doesn't mean pause and wait for God to speak in an audible voice to you. Hearing God's voice can be a thought that the Holy Spirit drops into your mind, or a leading in your spirit that's similar to a "gut feeling."

James 5:16 – *"...The earnest (heartfelt, continued) prayer of a righteous man makes tremendous power available [dynamic in its working]."* (AMPC)

Prayer makes the power of God available to us in the situations we're facing. It also keeps us trusting in and relying on Him for whatever we need. That's why it's essential that it's a part of our everyday life.

In Matthew 6:9-15, Jesus gave us a model for how we should pray. You probably know or have heard these verses because they are often called "The Lord's Prayer."

- Worship – I begin by expressing my love to God. *"Our Father in heaven, hallowed be your name..."*
- Surrender – I commit myself to doing God's will in every area of my life. *"Your kingdom come, your will be done, on earth as it is in heaven..."*
- Provision – I ask God to provide for my daily needs. *"Give us today our daily bread..."*
- Forgiveness – I ask God to forgive my sins and I forgive others. *"Forgive us our debts as we have also forgiven our debtors."*
- Protection – I ask for protection over my life. *"And lead us not into temptation but deliver us from the evil one."*

You can pray anywhere, but it's also important to make sure that you're setting aside a specific time each day to pray. There are no rules to how long or short it has to be; start small and just tell God what is on your mind. Having a strong daily prayer life keeps us spiritually vibrant and connected to God. It produces a kind of intimacy, power and depth to our relationship with God that can't be found in any other way.

Worshiping

Psalm 100:1-2, 4 – *"Shout with joy to the Lord, all the earth! Worship the Lord with gladness. Come before him, singing with joy...Enter his gates with thanksgiving; go into his courts with praise."* (NLT)

The third habit that should be present in every believer's life is worship. Worship is simply expressing our love and devotion to God from the inside out. Worship comes from our heart and mind and is expressed with our soul and our strength. It's not just mentally being focused on God, being spiritually committed to Him, or singing songs to Him – instead, worship is an attitude of the heart, something that radiates from every fiber of our being.

The Bible says in Mark 12:30, *"Love the Lord God with all your heart and with all your soul and with all your mind and with all your strength."* Worship spans the entirety of our being – physically, emotionally, mentally and spiritually. This idea may take you out of your comfort zone, especially when it comes to worshiping God with your physical being. The Bible is full of verses that tell us God wants us to praise Him and worship Him with the physical body He gave us. Here are six ways we can worship:

- Singing
  Psalm 30:4 – *"Sing to the Lord, all you godly ones!"* (NLT)
- Shouting
  Psalm 66:1 – *"Shout joyful praises to God, all the earth!"* (NLT)
- Clapping my hands
  Psalm 47:1 – *"Clap your hands! Shout to God with joyful praise!"* (NLT)
- Dancing
  Psalm 149:3 – *"Praise his name with dancing..."* (NLT)
- Lifting up my hands
  Psalm 134:2 – *"Lift up your hands in the sanctuary..."*
- Lifting up my voice
  Acts 4:24 – *"When they heard this, they raised their voices together in prayer to God..."*

Worship can take place in two different contexts: corporate and personal. Corporate worship is when we spend time worshiping God together with other believers in the setting of a local church. Personal worship is when we connect with God personally through worship, usually in a daily quiet time.

Worship in each of these contexts brings something unique and significant into our relationship with God. They both play a role in our spiritual growth, so it's important that we make sure we're in church, worshiping with other believers and also take time to worship God on a daily basis to experience Him in a personal way.

Fasting

Fasting is something you may not be very familiar with, but it's a powerful spiritual discipline that was practiced in Bible times and is still practiced today by Christians. Fasting is talked about throughout the Bible, and Jesus fasted during His time on earth. Fasting is simply giving up food, or other things like television, for a period of time for spiritual purposes. One of the reasons fasting is so powerful is that it pushes our flesh down so that our spirit can grow stronger. "The flesh" refers to the physical and emotional desires of our human nature, also referred to as our "natural man." Fasting helps weaken the grip of the flesh over our life and frees us to focus wholly on strengthening our spirit man.

Why We Fast

- To stay in tune with God and remain sensitized to the Holy Spirit.
- For miracles and supernatural breakthrough.
- To keep our flesh weak and our spirit strong.
- To see bondages broken in our lives – strongholds, addictions and negative habits (spiritual, physical, emotional or relational).
- To receive healing and restoration.
- To prepare us for new seasons ahead.

Kinds of Fasts

In the Bible we find different types of fasts. The complete fast is when you go without food or drink of any kind and should be done for a very limited time period. A regular fast is when you give up all food. On this type of fast, it's important to drink lots of water, juices and broths. The partial fast is when you give up certain foods or drinks, like meats and sweets, for an extended period of time. We see this fast in the book of Daniel, which is why it is also called a Daniel fast.

Whatever fast you choose to do, go for it wholeheartedly with a passion to experience God in a brand new way. God is not as concerned with what you do as much as the heart behind it. If it's a sacrifice to you, that's what matters to Him. Fasting has been one of the most powerful spiritual catalysts in my life. It's not easy and requires a lot of discipline, but the rewards it brings are absolutely worth it.

Practical Tips for Fasting

- Have a clear goal – what are you fasting for?
- Prepare spiritually – are there any things in your life that could keep you from hearing from God?
- Decide what to fast – if you've never fasted before, try starting by fasting one meal or by doing a partial fast.
- Prepare physically – check with your doctor and begin eating smaller portions. Begin eliminating caffeine and sugar from your diet.

Giving

The fifth habit that I want to encourage you to make a part of your Christian walk is giving. Many people struggle in the area of their finances. Their lives are plagued with stress, frustration, anxiety, fear, and they live constrained and limited by their finances.

God wants you to experience total freedom in every area of your life, including your finances. He came so that we could enjoy a full, overflowing life in every area (John 10:10). The Bible talks about money a lot - there are over 800 verses about it and it's talked about five times more than prayer. Obviously, God knew it would be something we'd need His insight on. We always experience His best for our lives when we do things His way, not ours.

How do we experience God's plan for financial freedom in our lives? There are three biblical principles that I believe have the potential to change your life and your financial situation as you regularly put them into practice.

1. Tithe consistently.
2. Manage responsibly.
3. Build a spirit of generosity.

When we devote ourselves to following God's principles and instructions, it brings freedom (Psalm 119:45). It's important to understand that these three steps are interrelated and interdependent. In other words, you can't follow one, but ignore the other two and expect it to produce the results promised in God's Word. You have to faithfully put all three into practice to receive the benefits and blessings God wants you to experience.

Step One: Tithe Consistently
Tithing is giving the first 10% of my income to God through my local church. This may be a completely new concept to you. Maybe you've heard of tithing, but thought it was more of a suggestion or an idea that the church came up with. The truth is, the principle of tithing comes straight from God and He instructs us to make tithing a regular part of our lives. It may not be easy to do at first, but obeying God's Word always brings blessings and benefits into our lives.

Malachi 3:10 – *"'Bring the whole tithe into the storehouse, that there may be food in my house. Test me in this,' says the Lord Almighty, 'and see if I will not throw open the floodgates of heaven and pour out so much blessing that you will not have room enough for it.'"*

In this verse we see there's our part and God's part. It's an "if/then" scenario: if we do our part (tithe), then He'll do His part (pour out blessing). But that means it starts with us. The ball is in our court to get things started!

Three Things to Remember About Tithing

- Tithing is giving God what belongs to Him.
  Leviticus 27:30 – *"One tenth of the produce of the land, whether grain from the fields or fruit from the trees, belongs to the Lord and must be set apart to him as holy."* (NLT)
- Tithing helps us put God first.
  Deuteronomy 14:23 – *"The purpose of tithing is to teach you always to put God first in your lives."* (TLB)
  Matthew 6:33 – *"...seek first his kingdom and his righteousness, and all these things will be given to you as well."*
- Tithing increases my faith in God.
  Malachi 3:10 – *"'...Test me in this,' says the Lord Almighty, 'and see if I will not throw open the floodgates of heaven and pour out so much blessing that you will not have room enough for it.'"*

Step Two: Manage Responsibly

After we lay a strong foundation for our finances by tithing consistently, it's important that we take the next step toward financial freedom and become responsible managers of what God has given us. We could also call this "stewardship." Stewardship simply means managing something that belongs to someone else.

Everything we have is from God (James 1:17) and therefore belongs to Him. So, we're really not the owners, we're just the managers of what we've been given. It's our job to take good care of what God has given us. We see in the Bible that good stewardship pays off. When we're faithful with a little, God can trust us with more (Matthew 25:14-30, Luke 16:10).

Practical Tips For Managing Finances Responsibly

- Know where your money is going (Proverbs 27:23).
- Live within your means (Proverbs 13:4).
- Work on getting rid of debt (Proverbs 22:7).
- Start saving, even if it's just a little (Proverbs13:11).

Step Three: Build a Spirit of Generosity

The third step we need to take to live in financial freedom is to build a generous spirit. Some people may think this is counterintuitive, but throughout His Word, God makes it clear that generosity should be a defining characteristic of a Christian's life (see Deuteronomy 15; 1 Timothy 6:18). We also see that that there are incredible blessings and favor that come to the person who chooses to live with a generous spirit. Proverbs 11:24 tells us, "The world of the generous gets larger and larger; the world of the stingy gets smaller and smaller. (MSG)

For many people, a generous spirit is the missing link in their approach to finances. Having a generous spirit isn't just about giving away large sums of money; it's more about the attitude of our hearts and minds. It's choosing to live openhanded, rather than tightfisted. When we have a generous spirit, it spills over into every area of our lives. It shows up in our attitude toward people, the words we speak and the way we give of our time, talent and treasure.

If you think about it, generosity is the essence of godliness. John 3:16 tells us God loved the world so much that He gave His son Jesus to die for our sins. If we're going to be like Christ, we need to be generous in every area of our lives.

These three principles are the foundation for managing finances God's way and experiencing true freedom and peace in this area of our lives. Whatever your next step is in this area, I encourage you to take it — don't wait.

If you are already consistently tithing, keep it up! You're right on track. If this concept of tithing is completely new to you, or if you used to tithe but haven't made it a regular practice in your life, I encourage you to take a step of faith and begin tithing consistently to your local church. Try it for 90 days and see what God does in your life. I'm confident that as you begin putting these three principles to work, you'll begin to move toward financial freedom and experience God's blessing in your life!

If you'd like more information on managing finances God's way, I wrote a short book on this topic called *Worry Free Finances*, available at johnsiebeling.com.

Serving

The sixth and final habit we're going to talk about is serving. There is something so significant and so powerful about doing things for other people. When we look at Jesus' life, we see that He lived His entire life with other people in mind. He was always teaching, healing, leading, even correcting, so that people would be lifted to a higher level in life. Jesus was the ultimate example of serving.

Matthew 20:28 – *"...the Son of Man came not to be waited on but to serve..."* (AMPC)

Serving is simply giving of yourself to make life better for someone else. If we want to be like Jesus, serving will be a way of life for us. Authentic, Christ-like serving starts in the heart.

It's an attitude and a perspective on life that says, *What can I do to make a difference for someone else?*

We've each been given unique gifts and talents. God hand-crafted you and made you exactly how He wanted you. It wasn't just so that you could benefit from your gifts. We see in these two passages of scripture that the purpose of those gifts and talents is to serve others and build the Body of Christ.

1 Peter 4:10 – *"God has given each of you some special abilities; be sure to use them to help each other, passing on to others God's many kinds of blessing."* (TLB)

1 Corinthians 12:5-7, 27 – *"There are different ways to serve the same Lord, and we can each do different things. Yet the same God works in all of us and helps us in everything we do. The Spirit has given each of us a special way of serving others...Together you are the body of Christ. Each one of you is part of his body."* (CEV)

The local church is the vehicle that God uses to share His love with the world. We have the amazing opportunity to be a part of that through serving. It could be as simple as greeting people with a friendly smile at the door or helping clean the building. You don't have to be super spiritual, incredibly talented or aspiring to full-time ministry to serve in God's House. Being available and having a willing heart is all it takes. There's a place for each of us to make a difference through serving in the House of God!

Over the years, serving has brought so many blessings into my own life. When we serve in our local church, not only do we build God's House, but it also brings benefits into our lives as well. It's a spiritual principle that when we sow good things, we'll reap the benefits in our lives.

Proverbs 11:25 – *"A generous man will prosper; he who refreshes others will himself be refreshed."*

A great benefit that comes into our lives through serving is the relationships we build. Some of the most incredible relationships that I have in my life today have come through serving in God's House. It's a great way to make friends who are heading in the same direction and are passionate about the things of God.

Another benefit that comes into our lives when we serve is spiritual growth and maturity. It expands our capacity, develops our gifts – even reveals new ones –

and it gives us opportunities to put what we're learning from God into practice.

Serving is also one of the best ways to get involved and make the church really feel like your church. I can't tell you how many people have shared stories of how their lives were changed when they began to serve in church. There's nothing more rewarding than devoting your time and energy to a cause that is impacting people's lives for eternity. When we take care of the things that are important to God, like serving people and building His House, He takes care of our lives better than we ever could on our own.

Make a decision to be someone who is generous with your time, energy and resources when it comes to serving God's House. Jump in, get involved and start serving with passion. As you do, I know that you'll experience God's blessings in your life.

Key Scriptures

Reading the Bible

Psalm 119

Matthew 4:4

Romans 10:17

2 Timothy 3:16-17

2 Peter 1:3

Praying

Psalm 17:6

Matthew 6:9-15

John 15:7-8

Philippians 4:6

James 5:16

1 John 5:14-15

Worshiping

Psalm 30:4

Psalm 47:1

Psalm 66:1

Psalm 100

Psalm 134:2

Psalm 149:3

Mark 12:30

Acts 4:24

Fasting

Esther 4

Daniel 9:2-4

Matthew 4:1-4

Matthew 6:16-18

Luke 2:36-38

Acts 13:2

Giving

Leviticus 27:30

Deuteronomy 14:23

Deuteronomy 15

Proverbs 11:17

Proverbs 11:24-26

Proverbs 13:11

Proverbs 13:11

Proverbs 22:7

Proverbs 27:23

Malachi 3:10

Matthhew 6:33

Matthew 25:14-30

Luke 16:10

John 10:10

John 3:16

1 Timothy 6:17-19

James 1:17

Serving

Proverbs 11:25

Matthew 20:28

1 Corinthians 12:5-7, 27

Ephesians 2:10

Ephesians 4:16

Philippians 2:3

1 Peter 4:10

Questions

1. Which of the six habits needs the most development in your life?

2. What is one small step that you can take today to begin establishing some of these habits in your life?

3. What old habits do you need to get rid of to make room for new habits in your life?

The Holy Spirit Today

THE HOLY SPIRIT TODAY

Throughout our journey as Christians, we'll face a wide variety of experiences and situations. There will be "mountaintop" experiences, full of joy and victory, and there will be "valley" experiences where we face challenges and our faith is tested. The awesome thing is, God promises to be with us every step of the way. He knew we'd need guidance to make decisions, comfort when our hearts are heavy, and correction to help us stay on course. That's why He gave us the Holy Spirit.

John 14:16 – "*...I will ask the Father to send you the Holy Spirit who will help you and always be with you.*" (CEV)

Who is the Holy Spirit?

The Holy Spirit is a Person

How do we know? Think about some of the qualities and characteristics you and I have as people: we have a mind, emotions and a will. We see from God's Word that the Holy Spirit has these qualities as well.

Romans 8:27 tells us the Holy Spirit has a mind: *"And he who searches our hearts knows the mind of the Spirit..."*

Ephesians 4:30 shows us He has emotions: *"And do*

not grieve the Holy Spirit of God, with whom you were sealed for the day of redemption."

I Corinthians 12:11 talks about His will: *"But one and the same Spirit works all these things, distributing to each one individually as He wills." (NASB)*

The Holy Spirit is God

The Holy Spirit is not part-God, but fully God. There is one God, eternally existing in three equal persons: Father, Son (Jesus Christ) and Holy Spirit. Our God is a triune God, meaning He is three in one. Jesus speaks of His Father and the Holy Spirit distinctly in John 14:26, when He says, *"The Helper, the Holy Spirit, whom the father will send in my name, He will teach you all things, and bring to your remembrance all that I said to you."* Also, the Apostle Paul prayerfully closes the book of 2 Corinthians by asking for *"the grace of the Lord Jesus Christ, and the love of God, and the fellowship of the Holy Spirit be with you all."*

The Holy Spirit is the Person of God in the Now

Once Jesus died on the cross for our sins and rose again on the third day, He had complete victory over sin and death. He then ascended into Heaven so that the Holy Spirit could come down and dwell within all believers.

That means that He is always with us, strengthening, comforting and leading us every moment of our lives. He is the person of God in the now and He lives inside of us! 1 Corinthians 3:16 says, *"Don't you know that you yourselves are God's temple and that God's Spirit lives in you?"* This verse tells us that if we are a believer, the Holy Spirit lives inside of us.

Some would say that's the extent of His role – He's kind of a silent presence in our lives that nudges our conscience now and then. However, if we really examine God's Word, we find there is more. Jesus spent quite a bit of time in the last months of His life teaching the disciples about the Holy Spirit. He knew how important it would be for them to have the Holy Spirit in their lives once He had gone.

In John 14:15-18, He told the twelve disciples: *"If you love Me, keep My commandments. And I will pray the Father, and He will give you another Helper, that He may abide with you forever – the Spirit of truth, whom the world cannot receive, because it neither sees Him nor knows Him; but you know Him, for He dwells with you and will be in you. I will not leave you orphans; I will come to you."* (NKJV)

I encourage you to take some time and read through John, the fourth book of the New Testament, chapters 14-17, to learn more about what Jesus said about the Holy Spirit. Reading these chapters will inspire you to allow the Holy Spirit to be a part of your everyday life.

What is the Baptism with the Holy Spirit?

Many people wonder where the expression "baptized with the Holy Spirit" comes from. Jesus was the first one to say it, and His words are recorded in the book of Acts, Chapter 1. After Jesus died and rose from the dead, one of the last things He instructed His followers to do was to wait in Jerusalem for the gift that His Father promised. He then said, "*...John baptized with water, but in a few days you will be baptized with the Holy Spirit.*" (Acts 1:4-5)

Let's put a definition to this term "*baptized with the Holy Spirit.*" The word baptize essentially means "to immerse." Holy Spirit baptism is an infilling experience that takes place when we open our lives to God without reservation, and we ask Him to baptize (immerse) us with His Holy Spirit.

What happens when we live a Spirit-led life?

When we're filled with the Spirit, there are some specific results that we'll begin to experience in our lives. These are some of the results that were evident in Jesus' life:

Direction

Luke 4:1 – "*Jesus, full of the Holy Spirit, returned from the Jordan and was led by the Spirit...*"

The first result of a Spirit-filled life is pretty clear and amazing – Jesus was led by the Holy Spirit. I think one of the greatest benefits of the Holy Spirit is that He gives our lives direction. We don't need to live in confusion or have a sense of hesitation surrounding our lives. We can walk in confidence and boldness, knowing that the Holy Spirit is directing our steps.

Power

Luke 4:14 – "*Jesus returned to Galilee in the power of the Spirit...*"

The second result of Spirit-filled living is power. Later, in the book of Acts, Jesus tells His disciples about this characteristic in Acts 1:8, "*But you will receive power when the Holy Spirit comes on you...*"

The power of the Holy Spirit enables us to do three important things: to live out our faith in front of friends and family, to overcome the challenges and problems we're facing, and to live the full, flourishing life that Jesus promised.

The effects and results of the Holy Spirit should impact our daily lives – not just our Sunday, but our Monday, Tuesday, Wednesday, Thursday, Friday and Saturday. I like to say it this way: the power of God is not only powerful, but also practical.

Purpose
Luke 4:18 – "*The Spirit of the Lord is on me, because he has anointed me to preach good news to the poor. He has sent me to proclaim freedom for the prisoners and recovery of sight for the blind, to release the oppressed...*"

There is a reason for the direction and power beyond just making life better for you.

There are a few important words in this famous passage in Luke:

because – this literally means "for the cause." God put His Spirit on Jesus for the cause of bringing hope, freedom and restoration to all people. There is always a "because" when the Holy Spirit is moving in your life!

anointed – here it literally means "to be covered with the Holy Spirit." When we are anointed, or covered with the Holy Spirit, we are empowered to accomplish what would be beyond our ability in the natural. The anointing helps us accomplish what God has called us to do.

Jesus was anointed for a purpose. In fact, this passage clearly says He was anointed to help people – the poor, the prisoners, the blind and the oppressed. A clear result of being Spirit-filled is you will be "others" focused. A good test of your Spirit-filled life is to ask yourself, *Am I living my life to serve and help other people*? The power of the Holy Spirit will enable you to fulfill God's purpose for your life. Ultimately, that purpose will be about helping others.

Jesus told His disciples in Acts 1:8 to wait in Jerusalem until the power of the Holy Spirit came into their lives. He explained that the Holy Spirit was coming to give them power to be witnesses for Him. We see power and purpose working together. There is a purpose for the power and it is to impact other people.

Spiritual Gifts

God gives us spiritual gifts to strengthen and build up the body of Christ. God has given you a unique set of spiritual gifts that help you contribute to the body as a whole. As we release our gifts, the body of Christ is strengthened and equipped to help people.

1 Corinthians 12:4-11 – "*There are different kinds of spiritual gifts, but the same Spirit is the source of them all. There are different kinds of service, but we serve the same Lord. God works in different ways, but it is the same God who does the work in all of us. A spiritual gift is given to each of us so we can help each other. To one person the Spirit gives the ability to give wise advice; to another the same Spirit gives a message of special knowledge. The same Spirit gives great faith to another, and to someone else the one Spirit gives the gift of healing. He gives one person the power to perform miracles, and another the ability to prophesy. He gives someone else the ability to discern whether a message is from the Spirit of God or from another spirit. Still another person is given the ability to speak in unknown languages, while another is given the ability to interpret what is being said. It is the one and only Spirit who distributes all these gifts. He alone decides which gift each person should have.*" (NLT)

Character Change

When the Holy Spirit is present in our lives, an internal transformation begins to take place in our mind, spirit and soul. He empowers us to develop the kind of character that God desires us to have. The Holy Spirit also helps us overcome the power of sin and live a life of freedom and victory.

Galatians 5:22-23 – "*But the Holy Spirit produces this kind of fruit in our lives: love, joy, peace, patience, kindness, goodness, faithfulness, gentleness, and self-control.*" (NLT)

Romans 8:2 – "*And because you belong to him, the power of the life-giving Spirit has freed you from the power of sin that leads to death.*" (NLT)

In order to please God with our lives and experience the fullness of His plan for us as believers, we need the Holy Spirit at work on the inside of us.

As a Spirit-filled Christian you need to believe God for these results in your life. Look for them and expect them as you walk out the life God has called you to live!

How Do I Receive the Gift of the Holy Spirit?

Jesus used the term baptism when referring to the disciples receiving the Holy Spirit in their lives. In studying Acts 1 we see that baptism with the

Holy Spirit is an experience distinct from salvation, although it can occur simultaneously. We find that baptism with the Holy Spirit was a normal and expected experience in New Testament times, and that the experience is for everyone who has accepted Jesus in our present day. It is clear in scripture that confessing Jesus as Lord of your life for salvation is the work of the Holy Spirit's presence in our lives. However, we also see that we should continually pursue the Holy Spirit to fill our lives. If you desire more of His presence in your life, begin with these steps:

1. Remove all barriers.

Things like anger, unforgiveness or other sins will keep us from receiving this great gift. It's important that we remove things in our lives that could block us from connecting with God freely.

Acts 2:38 – *Peter replied, "Repent and be baptized, every one of you, in the name of Jesus Christ for the forgiveness of your sins. And you will receive the gift of the Holy Spirit."*

2. Request the Holy Spirit.

God desires to give us good gifts and the Holy Spirit is one of the greatest gifts He offers us. The Bible tells us that if we ask, God will gladly give us the Holy Spirit.

Luke 11:11-13 – "*Now suppose one of your fathers is asked by his son for a fish; he will not give him a snake instead of a fish, will he? Or if he is asked for an egg, he will not give him a scorpion, will he? If you then, being evil, know how to give good gifts to your children, how much more will your heavenly Father give the Holy Spirit to those who ask Him?*"

3. Release the gifts.
Step out in faith and begin exercising the gifts that come as a result of the Holy Spirit's presence in your life. As you do, you'll be strengthened and built up in your own life and be equipped to serve those around you.

1 Peter 4:10 – "*Each one should use whatever gift he has received to serve others, faithfully administering God's grace in its various forms.*"

Prayer for the Baptism with the Holy Spirit
Here is a simple prayer to help you get started:
Father, I come to you in the name of Jesus. I'm hungry for all that you have for me. Your Word promises that those who hunger will be filled. I believe that it is your

will to give me this great gift of the baptism with the Holy Spirit. I ask you to forgive me of my sin (confess specifically anything that's on your heart or mind). I know your heart toward me is good and you only want to give me good things, so I receive it by faith right now. Baptize me and fill me with the Holy Spirit. In Jesus' name, amen.

The Holy Spirit is an incredible gift God has given us so that we have guidance and a comforter through every situation we face. This chapter shares just the beginning of how the Holy Spirit can work in your everyday life. If you'd like to learn more, *The Holy Spirit Today* is a short, easy-to-read book that goes more in depth to explain the Holy Spirit's role in our lives. You can purchase *The Holy Spirit Today* at johnsiebeling.com.

Key Scriptures

Luke 4:1

Luke 4:14

Luke 4:18

Luke 24:49

John 14:15-18

Acts 1:4-5

Acts 1:8

Acts 2:1-21, 37-39

Acts 8:4-8

Acts 10:44-48

Acts 19:1-7

Romans 8:26-27

1 Corinthians 3:16

1 Corinthians 12:11

1 Corinthians 14

Ephesians 4:30

Ephesians 5:18-19

Jude 20

Questions

1. Do you have thoughts or mindsets about the Holy Spirit that don't line up with God's Word?

2. What are some areas in your life that could benefit from the Holy Spirit's working in a greater way?

3. Are there barriers in your heart or mind that you know you need to deal with? Things like unforgiveness, sin, fear or uncertainty about the Holy Spirit could hinder you from fully experiencing this awesome gift of the baptism with the Holy Spirit.

Who Are You Running With?

WHO ARE YOU RUNNING WITH?

The Bible has a lot to say about relationships and the fact that the people we choose to run with will play a major part in shaping our lives. One of my favorite verses in the Bible that shows the significance of our relationships is found in the book of Ephesians, which was written originally as a letter by the Apostle Paul to the church in the city of Ephesus. The whole book of Ephesians really focuses on the power of the body of Christ, especially local churches around the world.

Ephesians 4:16 – *"From whom the whole body, joined and knit together by what every joint supplies, according to the effective working by which every part does its share, causes growth of the body for the edifying of itself in love."* (NKJV)

Let's think about some things in this verse. First, it pretty clearly indicates that it's God's desire that we are joined, connected and knit together in different relationships. Second, every relationship brings supply into our life. This is the most important thought in this verse: *What kind of supply is coming into my life through my relationships?* Think about your friends and ask yourself this question, *What are they supplying to my life?* Be honest. Is it good supply? You also have to think about what kind of supply is flowing from you to them. Thirdly, this verse clearly tells us that relationships are the key source of growth and maturity in our life.

The people we're connected with greatly influence where our lives are headed. They can either speak life and help you become all that God created you to be, or they can weigh you down and hinder you from accomplishing your purpose in life. When you make a fresh start, there might be some relationships you know you need to end. This doesn't mean you have to cut yourself off from all of your friends, co-workers and family members who aren't Christians.

Instead, look for opportunities to share what He's done in your life and help others come to know Him, too. Here's an important key when it comes to navigating the relationships in your life: give the right people the right voice in your life. You don't need to isolate yourself, but you also need to be careful about who is influencing your life. Make sure your pastors, leaders and Christian friends who are on track with God are the ones who hold a place of influence. The people we give a voice to will play a huge role in determining the direction of our lives.

Stop and Think About Who You're Running With

Since this is such an important area of our life, it's probably a good idea to stop and take inventory of our key relationships. I'm not really talking about acquaintances or those you see and interact with every now and then. Take a look around at your friends, the people who are influencing you.

When I first became a Christian, I heard that God had a purpose for me and it changed my life. You may have heard something similar and it is true - God has an incredible purpose and plan for you, too. Jeremiah 29:11 says, *"'For I know the plans I have for you,' declares the Lord, 'plans to prosper you and not to harm you, plans to give you hope and a future.'"* As Christians, our greatest responsibility and highest privilege is to please God and honor Him with our lives. The term "Christian" means not only that you are a follower of Christ, but an ambassador and a representative for Christ. Every decision, including your relationships, needs to pass the litmus test of purpose. *Will this serve God's purposes in my life? Does this please God? Am I honoring God through this? Is my life moving forward into the future God has for me?* If we want to become all that God wants us to be and accomplish all He has for us to do, our relationships must line up with His purpose for our lives.

That might mean making some tough decisions when it comes to friends and relationships. Over the years, there have been times when I had to choose to keep pursuing God and His plans for my life, even though it meant losing friends who were running in another direction. If there are people who are pulling you away from your commitment to Jesus and His Church, pulling you away from what God encourages in His Word, then you're going to have to make some difficult decisions about what's important to you. There will be relationships along the way that you will have to let go of in order to be who God has called you to be and do what God has called you to do. You might even feel a little tugging right now about a friend or someone you're involved with. You may be thinking that you're supposed to stay connected with them because of what I talked about earlier – so that you can be the supply of God's love to them.

We should always have a heart that is soft toward those in need of God's love and we should have a burden to reach them. However, there is a difference between being an example of God's love to your unsaved friends and holding onto relationships that are dragging you down and keeping you from growing in your walk with God. Unfortunately, I have seen people get pulled down because they stayed connected with the wrong friends.

The Bible warns us in 1 Corinthians 15:33, *"Don't be misled: Bad company corrupts good character."* Ask the Holy Spirit to give you wisdom and direction about the relationships in your life.

As you grow stronger in your walk with God, He will bring people into your life so you can encourage them and help them learn about the things of God. We should each have a drive and a desire to help the people in our lives experience the same amazing God that we know and serve. It's what we're called to do as believers! However, it should never come at the cost of compromising your own relationship with Christ. Especially in the early stages of your walk with Jesus, you've got to make sure that you're surrounding yourself with strong, godly people who are helping you get established in God's Word. It will enable you stay spiritually strong and healthy, and that is what makes us able to effectively share God's love with those around us.

Don't Isolate Yourself

As important as it is to make sure you're running with the right people, it's equally as important to make sure you don't isolate yourself. Proverbs 18:1 tells us, *"A man who isolates himself seeks his own desire; He rages against all wise judgment."* (NKJV)

One of the reasons being part of a healthy, life-giving local church is so significant in a believer's life is it means we don't have to do life alone. The local church gives us a place to find godly friends and be a part of a church family. Those relationships provide strength in difficult times. They encourage us and help us be better Christians and individuals. They make life sweeter and richer. Nothing can compare to having friends who are headed in the same direction as you and share the same commitment to God.

Make a decision to be friendly. This might sound so simple and maybe even somewhat silly. The reality is that sometimes we can get so busy, weighed down with worry, or overly serious that we forget the importance of simply being friendly.

Proverbs 18:24 – *"A man who has friends must himself be friendly..."* (NKJV)

Diversity

I think it's important to intentionally build relationships with people who are different from you. One of the things I love the most about the Body of Christ is the diversity. Think about the three ways you relate with people...

You Relate Up

The Bible is clear that we need to submit ourselves to authority. God is the one who has established governments and those in authority.

Romans 13:1 – *"Everyone must submit himself to the governing authorities, for there is no authority except that which God has established. The authorities that exist have been established by God."*

This verse obviously speaks of those in governmental and civic leadership, but also includes our supervisors at work, our teachers, our parents and those in spiritual leadership of our local church.

Hebrews 13:17 – *"Obey your leaders and submit to their authority. They keep watch over you as men who must give account. Obey them so that their work will be a joy, not a burden, for that would be of no advantage to you."*

Some people have a really hard time submitting to authority. They're always resisting those who are trying to lead and guide them. If this is something that is difficult for you, pray that God would give you a soft, pliable heart. It's impossible to grow and thrive spiritually with a hard, rebellious heart toward those who are in authority over us.

You Relate Side-to-Side

These are your friends, the people who are walking with you. I'm so thankful for all of the amazing friends that God has brought into my life. They encourage me, challenge me, and hold me accountable to goals and commitments I've made. I really believe true wealth isn't found in our possessions or how much money we have, but in relationships. It takes time and hard work to build great, healthy, life-giving friendships, but it's worth it. Great friendships are a two-way street. You have to invest in the relationship and so does the other person. Make sure you do your part. Don't just receive; determine to be a giver in your relationships.

You Relate Down

I don't mean that anyone is beneath you, but there are those who are coming behind you in life and in the things of God. There will always be people ahead of you and those behind you, and one of the greatest things you can do is take responsibility to help encourage and lead others. This happens as soon as we become Christians. We can tell people what has happened in our life and it will impact them. Then, as you grow in your knowledge of the Bible and the things of God, you will have the opportunity to influence and help others grow.

We receive great teaching, learn about the things of God and grow spiritually so that we can turn around and help other people. God will bring people in your life that He wants you to love and encourage. Always remember this: spiritual maturity isn't measured by what you know, nor does it automatically come with age or how long you've been a Christian. Spiritual maturity comes when you accept responsibility to grow personally and to help others grow.

Serve Others

I think this is one of the most important qualities of Christianity. One of my favorite examples is when Jesus washed the feet of His disciples. You can read about it in John 13. In Jesus' day, everyone walked barefoot or in sandals, so when you got home after being out, or if you were visiting someone's house, it was customary that your feet would be washed. Obviously this wasn't a very pleasant task, and therefore it was always reserved for the lowest servant in the house. When Jesus washed the feet of His disciples He was setting an example for them and for us – always be ready to serve and do the jobs no one else wants to do.

John 13:14-15 – *"Now that I, your Lord and Teacher, have washed your feet, you should also wash one another's feet. I have set you an example that you should do as I have done for you."*

Mark 10:43-45 – *"...whoever wants to become great among you must be your servant, and whoever wants to be first must be slave of all. For even the Son of Man did not come to be served, but to serve..."*

One of the most practical and important ways to build relationships is by getting involved. Serving others faithfully will make a huge difference in your life.

1 Peter 4:10 – *"Each one should use whatever gift he has received to serve others, faithfully administering God's grace in its various forms."*

Key Scriptures

Proverbs 15:22
Proverbs 18:1
Proverbs 18:24
Proverbs 27:17
Ecclesiastes 4:8-12
Jeremiah 29:11
Mark 10:43-45
John 13:14-15
Romans 13:1
1 Corinthians 15:33
Ephesians 4:16
Hebrews 13:17
1 Peter 4:10

Questions

1. How are the current relationships in your life impacting you?

2. Are there changes that you need to make in how you relate to people?

3. What are some steps you need to take to make sure you're connected into a network of godly, healthy relationships?

In It To Win It

IN IT TO WIN IT

The Christian life is a journey, a process of becoming more and more like God. It's a marathon, not a sprint, and it's not necessarily how you start that counts, but how you finish. You need to make a commitment that you are not going to give up, no matter what. Decide now to keep pressing forward into all that God has for you and determine that you will finish strong.

Galatians 6:9 – *"Let us not become weary in doing good, for at the proper time we will reap a harvest if we do not give up."*

The truth is, there will be distractions and temptations along the way. You will make mistakes, even stumble and fall, but always remember that God is on your side, leading and strengthening you. He will always be right there helping you back up when you fall and encouraging you to keep going. There will be occasions in our walk with God when we will be tempted to quit and stop, but we have to keep moving forward, and when we do, the Bible teaches we will be rewarded.

Hebrews 10:36 – *"You need to persevere so that when you have done the will of God, you will receive what he has promised."*

Over and over again, the Bible encourages us to fight life through to the end.

Matthew 24:13 – *"...he who stands firm to the end will be saved."*

Hebrews 6:11 – *"We want each of you to show this same diligence to the very end, in order to make your hope sure."*

Attitude

When it comes to not giving up, I really believe our attitude, more than anything else, will determine our success. When we really commit to renewing our mind we will be confronted with different attitudes that have the potential to keep us from growing spiritually. We may not even be aware of these attitudes or mindsets until they pop up. Some of them we picked up from our family, and others came through experience. Every time we bump up against one of these attitudes or mindsets, it's an opportunity to allow God to change us. In fact, as you confront these attitudes and overcome them, it will be the greatest example to your friends and family because they will see the real change that Jesus has made in your life.

Here's something important to remember: spiritual maturity depends on spiritual freedom. The more you keep renewing your mind, the freer you will become. The freer you are, the more you will grow spiritually.

Ephesians 4:23 – *"...be made new in the attitude of your minds."*

Here are some of the attitudes we need to confront if we're going to walk in freedom, be all that God wants us to be, and do all that God wants us to do.

Fear

Fear might be the most significant attitude we will have to confront in our life because it's so prevalent in our culture. You have to remember, we do have an enemy, Satan, and one of his greatest tools against us is fear. Why? Because fear is the opposite of faith, and faith is the most powerful thing we have at our disposal.

Hebrews 11:6 – *"And without faith it is impossible to please God..."*

Think about that: if we don't have faith, we can't please God. Faith does not only enable us to believe that God exists, but it also enables us to trust God in our daily lives. Often we will have to press against fear and take the steps God is leading us to take. Faith isn't the absence of fear, but it is doing the right thing even if we're afraid. Fear shows itself in our lives as worry, anxiety and even frustration. We don't have to live in fear. We can trust God for anything and everything in our life.

Spiritual Arrogance

We can't let pride and arrogance take root in our hearts when we start learning the Bible and God begins blessing our lives. Just as pride is one of the most sinister attitudes we have to guard against, humility is one of the most powerful spiritual attitudes we can build in our lives.

1 Peter 5:5 – *"...All of you, clothe yourselves with humility toward one another, because, 'God opposes the proud but gives grace to the humble.'"*

It is our responsibility to humble ourselves. Humility is something we put on, like our clothes. When we put on humility, God gives us grace, which is His powerful, enabling and empowering presence in our lives. I believe we are "graced for our place." Have you ever watched someone walk through something really difficult and were amazed at how they stayed so strong? You may have even thought to yourself, "If that were me, there is no way I would be that strong." The truth is, it's God's grace flowing in their life. Grace is more than something we say before we eat. It is the powerful presence of God that can be part of our everyday life so we can stay strong no matter what we're facing. The passage we just read teaches that we can have God's grace if we remain humble.

Blame

Don't fall into the trap of blaming people or circumstances. Blame is so closely connected to our human nature. In the Garden of Eden, right at the moment when sin entered the world through the disobedience of Adam and Eve, blame was present. Adam blamed Eve and God, and Eve blamed the devil.

Genesis 3:12-13 – *"The man said, 'The woman you put here with me – she gave me some fruit from the tree, and I ate it.' Then the Lord God said to the woman, 'What is this you have done?' The woman said, 'The serpent deceived me, and I ate.'"*

Too many people are playing the blame game. A great way to get some momentum in your life is to stop making excuses and begin taking responsibility for where you are right now in life. If you fall, don't blame anyone or anything else. Take responsibility, and get back up. Remember what Proverbs 24:16 says, *"For though the righteous fall seven times, they rise again…"*.

Negativity

It's a simple fact that your attitude creates the environment of your life. If you think negative thoughts all the time, you will end up saying negative things. Negativity will surround you. Some people are just naturally negative. They're pessimistic, seeing the glass half-empty. Others become that way as a result of things that have happened in their lives. It's good to be practical and accept the truth, but you can accept the truth in a positive way. For many people, there is a spiritual root of negativity in their life. It's holding them back from God's best.

In Philippians 4:8-9, Paul encourages us to make sure that our minds are fixed on the positive, not the negative. *"Summing it all up, friends, I'd say you'll do best by filling your minds and meditating on things true, noble, reputable, authentic, compelling, gracious – the best, not the worst; the beautiful, not the ugly; things to praise, not things to curse. Put into practice what you learned from me, what you heard and saw and realized. Do that, and God, who makes everything work together, will work you into his most excellent harmonies."* (MSG)

Our thoughts and our words actually determine who we become and the kind of life we'll have (Proverbs 23:7, Proverbs 18:21), so make a commitment to be positive.

I think you'll be amazed at the benefits being positive can bring to your life. When you have a positive outlook, you'll experience a new level of freedom and joy. You'll look forward to the future because of all the possibility it holds, instead of dreading it because of all the bad things that might happen. You'll enjoy life and your relationships because you're not expecting the worst all the time. You'll dream bigger because you believe that great things can happen in your life! Most importantly, when you're committed to having a positive attitude no matter what, you are a source of hope and life to those around you. One of the most powerful and attractive qualities we can have as Christians is an optimistic, vibrant attitude toward life because we know that God is for us and has a great plan for our lives. In a world full of negativity, that's a sure way to make people take notice and say, "I want to be more like that!"

Complacency

The Bible says that we should always be fired up and passionate for God. In fact, one of my favorite verses in the Bible pretty much leaves us without excuse when it comes to the passion quotient in our life:

Romans 12:11 – *"Never be lacking in zeal, but keep your spiritual fervor, serving the Lord."*

That doesn't give us much of a way out. We should always be full of zeal and spiritual fervor. The word fervor literally means, "full of fire and passionate." Originally, the word passion was used to describe what Jesus suffered on the cross. What Jesus experienced was so incredible a new word was created to describe it. Jesus was a man of passion. He had intensity and was emotional (Matthew 9:35-38; Mark 3:1-6; Luke 10:21; John 2:13-17). He had compassion. He was full of joy. He was angry. He wept and was sad. As Christians we cannot justify living a life with no emotion, no passion, and no fire because it doesn't match up with the example Jesus gave us when He lived on earth. Some people even confuse this with personality. Being passionate doesn't really have anything to do with your personality. It's about your inner fire.

If you look up the word passion and then look for the antonym, the opposite, you'll find words like apathy, indifference and complacency. We must fight against this in our lives. The Bible warns us in Proverbs 1:32, *"For the waywardness of the simple will kill them, and the complacency of fools will destroy them."*

Complacency is simply a lack of passion. It's a "whatever" attitude. It's pretty clear in this verse that complacency is not only foolish, but it is destructive. I believe complacency destroys potential. So many people are gifted and have a great deal of potential, but because they don't care, they won't develop that potential and become all that God wants them to become. Complacency also destroys and shrinks our capacity to experience God in new and fresh ways.

Keep these five attitudes in mind, and remember to keep moving forward, fighting life through to the very end. The Apostle Paul called it *"the good fight of faith"* because it is a good fight. No matter where you are, I believe you have only just begun to see the incredible things God has in store for you. We don't have to struggle and barely survive, because God has called us to thrive in life.

The best is yet to come. Life can get better and better,

and we can get stronger and stronger because God is leading us and we're committed to become all that He wants us to become! When you feel like giving up, don't! Remember *"He will keep you strong to the end..."* (1 Corinthians 1:8).

Key Scrptures

Proverbs 18:21
Proverbs 23:7
Proverbs 24:16
Matthew 24:13
Galatians 6:9
Ephesians 4:23
Philippians 1:6
Philippians 4:8
Hebrews 6:11
Hebrews 10:36
Hebrews 11:6
1 Peter 5:5

Questions

1. Are there distractions and/or temptations you need to remove from your life to help make sure you're running your race well and are able to finish strong?

2. What changes do you need to make in your heart and attitude?

3. Do you have Godly people in your life who can encourage you when you feel discouraged or tempted to quit? Are you humble enough to ask for help?

ABOUT THE AUTHOR

John and Leslie Siebeling are the founding pastors of The Life Church based in Memphis, TN. Started in 1996 with just seven people, the church has grown into a thriving, multi-campus church with a diverse congregation numbering in the thousands. John's passion is to see people come to know Jesus and discover the flourishing life God has for them. His gift of teaching the truth of God's Word in a relevant way, transcending cultural, racial and social barriers, has made his weekly television broadcast a success. He is a lead team member for the ARC (Association of Related Churches), an organization that plants new churches throughout the United States. John and Leslie have two children, Anna and Mark. John is also the author of *Momentum, Worry Free Finances* and *Moving Forward: Overcoming the Habits, Hangups and Mishaps That Hold You Back.* To find out more about John and his resources, visit johnsiebeling.com.